HA T

GAN

EIDDIL IFOR
(Thomas Evan Watkins)
1834

TRANSCRIBED AND FOOTNOTES ADDED BY
COLONEL J.A. BRADNEY, C.B.

TOGETHER WITH AN ENGLISH TRANSLATION BY

THE REVEREND EVAN PRICE
(Ebbw Vale)

First published in this edition 1998
in association with the Llanfoist & District Historical Society

ISBN 1 872730 16 7

Illustrated by Michael Blackmore

BLORENGE •BOOKS•

Blorenge Cottage, Church Lane, Llanfoist
Abergavenny, Gwent, NP7 9NG. Tel: 01873 856114

Printed by Mid Wales Litho Ltd.,
Units 10 - 13, Pontyfelin Ind. Est.,
New Inn, Pontypool, Gwent NP4 ODQ
Tel: 01495 750033

INTRODUCTION

The author of the essay here printed was Thomas Evan Watkins, known in bardic circles as *Eiddil Ifor*, and later as *Ynyr Gwent*. He was born 1st May, 1801, in a cottage at a place called Pwll yr Hyward,* above Cwm Llanwenarth, near the Garnddyrys ironworks, in the parish of Llanfoist, his father being Thomas Evan Watkins (called Thomas Evan o'r Rhyd).

His grandfather was Evan Watkins of Blaenau Gwent (Evan o'r Rhyd), the son of David ap Hywel ap Thomas ap David Watkins, of the same stock as the families of Watkins of Ebbw Vale, of the Grug, of the Fedw Fawr, and of the Pwll in Llangwm. Evan and his wife Elizabeth, who was daughter of ... Jenkins of Cwm Llanwenarth, moved from Blaenau to Cwm Llanwenarth in 1763, their eldest child Thomas (father of Eiddil Ifor) being then a year old. Evan was a man given to bad habits, card playing, dancing, and to the fruit of Sir John Barleycorn (ffrwyth Syr Shon Heiddyn). He was a believer in spirits, corpse-candles, hobgoblins (y pwcciaid), and used to relate at the fireside stories of Jackey Kent (Sion Cent) and Twm Shon Catti. He died in April, 1812, aged 82. Thomas, his son, at the age of 18 (1780) had had next to no religious teaching, for though, as the writer says, very few people spoke English in or around Abergavenny, the services in the parish churches were nearly all in English. He went to hear Morgan Harris, the preacher at Llanwenarth Baptist Chapel, and there learnt to sing. After working for some time for Mr. Edmund James at Abertillery, he returned to Cwm Llanwenarth, and worked for Messrs. Hill and Hopkins, the proprietors of Blaenavon ironworks, in their limestone quarries at Pen Rhiw Ifor, living with his father and mother at Pwll yr Hwyaid. He then became a member at the chapel at Llanwenarth, and a devoted adherent and leader of the singing. About 1798 he married Miss Davies of Devynog, who became the mother of Eiddil Ifor and of seven other children. She died in 1813, and Thomas in 1815 married a second wife, Miss Ann Davies of Llandyfaelog Fach, by whom he had more children. Thomas died 8th May, 1842, aged 80. One of the daughters married Mr. James Edwards of the Coed, more properly called Coedeithin, Blaenavon, a freeholder of an ancient family.

---

*This is so spelt in the biographical account of his father by Eiddil Ifor in Y Gwir Fedyddiwr, Feb. 1843, but it is obviously an error for Pwll-yr-hwyaid (the ducks' pool). The notes given as to the ancestry of Eiddil Ifor are from this account.

Pwll du Howard (Pwll yr Hyward) the birthplace of Thomas Evan Watkins, was situated at the head of Cwm Llanwenarth, but very little of the building now remains.

As a young man Eiddil Ifor kept the White Hart Inn at Blaenavon. He soon went to Blaenau Gwent, and was employed as weigher in the machine office under the Levicks, the then proprietors of the ironworks there. Here he remained until about 1860. He then returned to Blaenavon, and kept the inn called the Three Cranes until he died.

His wife died in 1859 and was buried in the churchyard at Llanover, where her tombstone bears the following inscription:

Er cof am MARI LEWIS, gwraig
T.E. Watkins (Ynyr Gwent) yr hon
a fu farw Mawrth y 6ed, 1859, yn ngweithiau
Haiarn Cwm Celyn a'r Blaenau yn y swydd hon,
yn 53ain oed.
Hwyaf hun hun angau.

He had two daughters, Ceinwen, who died unmarried in 1885, and Mary, who married William Gwynn, a carpenter working for the Blaenavon Company. Mrs. Gwynn had two daughters who both predeceased their mother. One of these, Miss Ceinwen Gwynn, was an accomplished musician, and died in 1907. The other, Miss Mary Gwynn, died in 1914.

Eiddil Ifor died in 1889, and was buried with his daughter Ceinwen in the graveyard attached to Ebenezer Baptist Chapel, in the Llanover Road at Blaenavon, where is a stone with this inscription:

In Loving Memory of CEINWEN
the beloved daughter of
Thomas Evan Watkins (Ynyr Gwent)
and Mary his wife,
Who died June 3rd 1885,
Aged 38 years
Life's race well run,
Life's work well done,
Life's crown well won.
Now comes rest.

Hefyd am ei thad, THOMAS EVAN WATKINS
(Ynyr Gwent), Bardd wrth Fraint a Defawd
Beirdd Ynys Prydain.
Ganwyd Mai y cyntaf, 1801

Marw ar Ionawr 31ain, 1889
Mab, Brawd, Gwr, Tad mad, Cymydog -- o bwyll,
A Bardd and dalentog!
Athraw awen gaeth rywiog,
Roed yn y glyn oer dan glog.

His old friend Nathan Dyfed (Mr. Jonathan Reynolds of Merthyr) mourned his decease in the following lines, of which a portion appears on the tomb-stone:

Mab, brawd, gwr. tad mad, cymydog -- o bwyll,
A bardd aml dalentog;
Twr iaith -- glyw dawn tereithiog,
Roed yn y glyn oer dan glog.
Mor wir ag i'r marworyn -- gloew, nefawl
Gael nwyfiant diderfyn,
Yn groew gof rhag llwgr gwyfyn,
Pery ei glod uwch pau'r glyn.

On Friday, 22nd November, 1833, was founded "by five and twenty respectable and zealous Welshman" of Abergavenny and the neighbourhood, who met at the Swan Inn, kept by Mr. John Michael, the society known as *Cymdeithas Cymreigyddion y Fenni.* Of this society Eiddil Ifor was one of the founders, being appointed bard. The other officials were the Rev. John Evans, vicar of Llanover, president; Thomas Bevan, known as *Caradawc*, secretary; the Rev. Thomas Price, vicar of Cwmdu, known as *Carnhuanawc*, correspondent. The first Eisteddfod at Abergavenny was held under the auspices of the Cymreigyddion on 22nd November, 1834, and among the prizes offered was one for a history of Llanfoist. The essay here printed was the only one sent in, and to the author was awarded the prize.

The gentlemen above named were all literary men, imbued with love of their country, its language and traditions. The Rev. John Evans, the president, was secretary of the Welsh Manuscript Society, under the auspices of which were published the *Liber Landavensis*, *Cambro-British Saints*, and many other works of great value. Mr. Thomas Bevan, a native of Llangynidr, was master of the Abergavenny Workhouse, and though he did not publish anything, was an energetic secretary and did much to make the gatherings a success. The Rev. Thomas Price was the author of *Hanes Cymru*, the first history of Wales written in the Welsh language. He revived the use of the Welsh triple-stringed harp, and himself played on it. He helped Mr. Theophilus Jones in his *History of the County of 'Brecknock,* for which he drew the coats of arms.

Another who took a prominent part in all the proceedings of the society was Thomas Griffiths, who for the greater part of his life lived at Llanover as harpist to Lord and Lady Llanover. He was a native of Llangynidr and, owing to an accident when a child, was afflicted with blindness. He became one of the most skilled players on the harp and won many prizes at Eisteddfodau. He was known as *Cerddor y Dwyrain* . In 1869 he played by command before Queen Victoria at Buckingham Palace, and at Marlborough House before the Prince of Wales (afterwards King Edward VII.), by whom he was appointed Welsh Harper Extraordinary to His Royal Highness. His daughter Mrs. Richards, called *Pencerddes y De*, still lives at Llanover, and is an equally talented player on the harp as her father. She has won many prizes and has instructed many pupils in her art. She was one of those present at the funeral of Eiddil Ifor.

The prize won by Eiddil Ifor on 22nd November, 1834, was given by Mr. William Price of Abergavenny, to whom is addressed the following letter thanking him for his generosity: (*Seren Gomer*, 1835.)

DIOLCHGARWCH
I
W. PRICE, YSWAIN, CYFREITHYDDYN Y FENNI.

Mr. Gomer, --

Byddwch mor garedig, trwy gyfrwng eich *Seren* fad, a dychwclyd fy niolchgarwch gwrescaf idd y boneddig blaenorol, am ei Roddiongwerthfawr I Gymdeithas Cymreigyddion y fenni, iddeu rhoddi idd yr ymgeisiwr (neu yr ymgeiswyr) llwyddiannus am y Traethodau goreu ar y Testunau canlynol : -- Yn gyntaf, y Llyfr enwog hwnw, sef *Cambria Triumphans, or Britain in its perfect Lustre*, gan y dysgedig Percy Enderbie o Lantarnam, yn swydd Fynwy, am y Traethawd goreu o Hanes Glewysig, &c. sef y Tiroedd rhwng Wysg a Rhymwy, a adnabyddid gynt wrth yr enw Tywysogaeth Glewysg. Yn ail, *Caradoc's History of Wales, by Dr. Powell; and a Description of Wales, by Sir John Price, the History of Anglesey, &c.and the Memoirs of Owen Glyndyfrdwy*, Am y Desgrifiad goreu o Blwyf Llanffwyst, ynghyd ag Hanes yr hen Deuleuoedd urddasawl a fuant yn byw ynddo, &c., -- y cyfryw wobrwyon a roddwyd ar Gylchwyl y Gymdeithas, Tachwedd y 26ain, 1834. Bydded iddo fwynhau hir oes a dedwyddwcch, ac ni dderfydd ei glod a'i haelioni tuag at ei iaith a'i wlad, tra y byddo ar y ddaear. Dilyned Cymry y Dywysogaeth eu cyfaill yn ei weithredoedd daionus; a thrwy hyny y ceir mwy gorchestion etto wedi eu cyflawni gan y Cymdeithasau Cymroaidd.

Yr eiddoch, Syr, &c.

AELOD O'R GYMDEITHAS*

* Seren Gomer, Jan. 1835.

"Thanks to William Price, Esq., Solicitor, Abergavenny. Mr. Gomer, - Will you kindly, through the medium of your kindly *Star*, return my warmest thanks to the above gentleman for his valuable gifts to the Society of the Abergavenny Cymreigyddion to be awarded to the

For many years Eiddil Ifor competed at Eisteddfodau, winning many prizes and medals. He was also a contributor to Seren Gomer, to which he sent a series of articles on "Helwriaeth yr Hen Gymry." He also published in Y Bedyddiwr articles on "Hanes Beirdd a Llenorion Gwent a Morganwg."

He was a regular attendant at Sunday School, and in politics a Liberal. His collection of historical books was large, and after his death these were sold to various people by his daughter Mrs. Gwynn. This lady presented his medals, 13 in number, won at Eisteddfodau, to the Welsh Library, Cardiff.

Mr. William Price, whose name often occurs in the essay and who gave the prize which it received, was a member of an old family in Llanfoist, living for many years at the Mardy and at Glan-nant-y-llan. He was the son of Benjamin, the son of William Price, the latter dying at the Mardy in 1775. Mr. William Price, died in 1882 aged 83, and was buried at the Baptist Chapel in Llanwenarth. The manuscript came into the hands of his son, Mr. Octavius Price of Newent, by whose permission it is now published.

---

best competitor or competitors for the best essay on the following subjects:- (1) That renowned book, 'Cambria Triumphans, or Britain in its perfect lustre,' by the learned Percy Enderbie of Llantarnam, in the county of Monmouth, for the best Essay on 'The History of Glewysig, viz. the Lands between Usk and Rhymwy [Rhymney], anciently known as the Principality of Glewysg.'(2) 'Caradoc's History of Wales,' by Dr. Powell, and a Description of Wales, by Sir John Price, the History of Anglesey, &c. and the Memoirs of Owain Glyndyfrdwy, for the best Description of the Parish of Llanfoist, and the old noble Families who lived there. The above prizes were awarded at the first Annual Meeting of the Society on Nov. 26th, 1834. May he enjoy long life and happiness, and his fame and generosity to his language and country will continue to the end of life. Let the Welshmen of the Principality emulate their friend in his kindly deeds, and we shall have greater productions still from the Welsh Societies.

I am, Sir, &c., A MEMBER OF THE SOCIETY."

HISTORY OF LLANFOIST
(HANES LLANFOIST)

Translated into English

by the

Rev. Evan Price (Ieuan Gorwydd)

Ebbw Vale

HISTORY OF LLANFOIST

By the

Rev. Eiddil Ifor (Thomas Evan Watkins)

November 22nd 1834

An essay containing a history and description of the parish of Llanfoist near
Abergavenny in the County of Monmouth
with the old gentry who resided there.
One of the subjects given by the Abergavenny Cymreigyddion
for their first annual meeting, November 22nd, 1834.

(*A Literal Translation from the Welsh*)

Mr President and Gentlemen.

When considering this subject I find many difficulties in the way of doing it justice; however, be that as it may, I propose submitting to you the following observations, in the firm hope that a superior production may yet be seen on your table. And if this essay should be deemed worthy of publication, I crave of you the opportunity of previously revising it, because of the shortness of time at present to do it adequate justice.

The Parish of Llanfoist extends from the banks of the Usk to the banks of the Torfaen, and is surrounded by the parishes of Abergavenny, Llanwenarth, Llanelly, Aberystruth, Trevethin, Llanelen, &c. There are some who believe the name (Llanfoist) to be derived from Llan and ffos, or Llan (Church) in the trench or marsh. Others (such as *Willet in Stranger in Monmouthshire*, 46) think it is Llanfoyle, whilst others still ask if there is no better derivation than either of the above names, and whether it cannot be derived from Llan and Faustus (Latin), that is to say, the lucky or prosperous church. Or it may be from Fausta, the daughter of Gwrtheyrn Gwrthenau by his first wife (*Warrington*, 63) and if so it may be inferred that this church was built at or about the beginning of the 6th century (Welsh saints, 86), although I am not aware that it has any register older than other churches. When historical researches are made (see *William's History of Monmouth*, app. 194) we find the family of one William's of Llanfoist descended from lineage of Caradog Fraich Fras, Earl of Hereford, the Prince and owner of the fine territories between the Wye and the Severn, Lord of Dolorous Castle, and a Baron of the Order of the Round Table in the Time of King Arthur. And that one Gwgan ap Blethin ap

A present day view of Llanfoist Church

Ancient yew tree in Llanfoist Churchyard

Maynarch, Lord of Brecknock, married Gwenllian, the daughter and heiress of Phillip ap Gwys, Lord of Wiston, and I believe the Church was built in the time of Gwgan ap Blethin, as a token of regard for her grandfather (Viz. The grandfather of Gwgan's wife). It was easy to change Gwys into Ffwys, and corrupted more and more by others, doubling the F, so that scarcely anybody seeing the spelling of the word today by the Welsh and English would imagine that it had any connection with Gwys (Llanfoist !!)

I shall now make a journey over the parish. It stands in the Lordship of Abergavenny, and in the upper portion of the Hundred of Abergavenny in Monmouthshire, in the Diocese of Llandaff, and the Archbishop of Canterbury. It is a parish and parsonage lying one mile to the west of the town of Abergavenny, valued in the Kings Books at £7 4 4 ½, and the first fruits at £0 14 5. The patron is Lord Abergavenny (*Willet*). The river Usk is the boundary between it and the other parishes on the east, and Llanwenarth parish on the north, Aberystruth on the west, Trevethin on the south west, Llanover on the south and Llanellen on the south east, all in Monmouthshire. This church has been recently renovated, and is now very convenient and beautiful. The grave yard contains two or three yew trees, and old remnants of a period far back beyond either memory or tradition, and many pine trees have been recently planted here. There are many gravestones recording the departure and mortal remains of many of the old gentry that were renowned in their day. People come here in great crowds on palm Sunday to adorn the graves with flowers, showing their reverence for the mortal remains of their beloved relatives who rest in the silence of the valley in the cold embrace of death. It is a practice celebrated in song by the superbly gifted muse of Dafydd ap Gwilym:

When the flowers all their splendour show ,
And the smooth branches from the silence grow,
I bring the rose from the closes far,
In fields and forests brilliant as a star,
The pliant clover, with glittering gems in mass,
The joy and pride of the pasture grass,
At the Lord's great hour in their lovely bloom,
I lay them loyally on Ivor's tomb,"

Amongst the incumbents of the parish may be mentioned the Revs Evan Eustance,[1] Ioan Gwilym [2] and Charles Powell,[3] who died about the 7th of September, 1827. He was succeeded by the Reverend James Jenkins,[4] of Blaenavon, who was inducted here on the nomination of Lord Abergavenny in 1827. (See *Cambrian*, Dec. 1st). The present curate in charge is the Rev William Jones, one of the members of your Cymreigyddion Society, who at present frequently officiates at the Church in the old Welsh language, with credit to himself and to the general edification of others.

The adjoining village contains 80 dwelling houses, 6 public houses, 1 beer brewery held by Mr James Jones, who carries on an extensive business. There are here also a clothier, fruitier, gardeners, and all kinds of craftsmen, with many facilities for trade, such as the route of the mail coach, with the mail coach from London to Merthyr Tydfil running back and fore daily, and another ordinary coach three times a week. There are other general roads, such as the tramroad and canals to Llanelly, &c. And to Brecon, and down to Pontypool and Newport. There are here two Yards (or enclosures), where coal and lime are being sold, with which I shall deal with in their proper places.

The population of this parish in 1831 was 891, with many empowered to vote in the representation of the county, but they have not all been registered in this parish because of their claim to registration in other parishes.

I shall endeavour to give a more definitive account of this parish by making a descriptive tour of the old roads and mentioning others when we meet them. When passing from the Church to Tudor Bridge on the river Usk, near Abergavenny, there is a field on the right which was part of Maerdy Farm, but was sold to P. Vaughan, Esq., of Brecon. Having left the churchyard there is a road on the left hand leading to the village of Govilon in the parish of Llanwenarth, and onwards to the iron works of Llanelly, Breconshire, Nantyglo, Merthyr Tydfil, Crickhowell, &c. and on the right hand from the church there is a road leading for a few yards and then

---

1. Evan Eustance. M.A., Jesus College, Oxford, was a Glamorganshire man, and was instituted to the living of Abergavenny 20th June 1719. It is doubtful if he was ever Rector of Llanfoist. He died in 1775.

2. Ioan Gwilym. This was presumably the bardic name of John Williams, M.A. who was instituted to the living of Llanfoist 8th March 1780. He was also vicar of Abergavenny. He died in 1803.

3. Charles Powell, M.A., Son of William Powell, vicar of Llantilio Pertholey, was instituted 1st March 1804.

4. James Jenkins was instituted 30th October 1827 and died in 1849. He was son of the Rev. William Jenkins, a vicar of Mydrin and Brechfa, co. Carmarthen. He married Leah, only child heir of John Griffiths of Blaenavon, by whom he had an only child, Ann, wife of Robert Wheeley of the Pentre.

branching into two, the one on the right hand leading to the old mill of the Baily-du Manor house, Llanelen village, and the iron works of Blaenavon, Torfaen, &c., to which I shall refer again, while the other branch on the left leads to the Maerdy Farm, the land of which lies on both hands of the tourist, but was sold some few years ago in plots of various sizes to several buyers. One of the plots on the left hand side is in the ownership of Mr James Jones, brewer, Abergavenny, who built on it the afore-mentioned brewery, a commodious inn and several dwelling houses. The plot of land on the right hand side is owned by Thomas Hill,[5] Esq. & Co., who have built large lime kilns on it, and the rest is surrounded by high walls , and in the yard, coal &c. are sold to the farmers around. And for the purpose of bringing those materials here they went to the great expense of constructing a tramroad from their iron works at Blaenavon, Pwlldu Colliery, Maenglawdd lime stones, Blaencwm, Llanwenarth, together with their brewing foundry at Garnddyrys, from

Ancient stone stile giving access to Llanfoist Churchyard.

---

5. Thomas Hill, proprietor of the ironworks at Blaenavon. He died in 1868.

Churchyard Cross, Llanfoist

whence also their tramroad runs almost evenly with the edge of the Blorenge to the side of Cwmcraf, where pulleys, wheels and iron chains liberate the trams, loaded with coal, iron and limestone, down the terrible slope to their first resting station, where a similar apparatus dispatches them onwards to their second stage, and then another to the third on the Abergavenny and Brecon Canal bank, and likewise the loaded trams bring the empty ones up the steep heights on the side of Cwmcraf to the canal. Here they unload the trams and fill the boats with iron, &c. for the port of Newport-on-Usk, to meet the ships which sail from pole to pole to all the harbours of the habitable globe. But they bring most of the coal and limestones over the canal by one of the machines similar to those already described, pulled by horses to the Yard already mentioned.

The road we next see from the parish road is that of the mail coach of Merthyr and Abergavenny, which crosses the parish road, leaving Merthyr on the left and Abergavenny on the right hand, and on the right again we have another portion or Maerdy Farm in the ownership of Mr Thomas Kershaw, draper, where he has built an inn, called the New Inn, with several fine dwelling houses. Here the parish road is crossed by the tramroad of Llanvihangel and Hereford, which was constructed about the year 18..., and runs from the Abergavenny and Brecon Canal, from near the village of Govilon (mentioned before, on the left hand) to the town of Abergavenny and the city of Hereford. And on its left hand we find the old building of the Maerdy which is now an alehouse, known by the name of Waterloo. We think the name Maerdy was taken from "Maer," a governor, who possibly resided there, presiding over a court of law, with jurisdiction over some part of the neighbourhood. Or it may have been taken from Maerdy, milkhouse. But I am rather disposed to believe the name was taken from the probability of the place being used in olden times as a court where legal complaints were brought before the chief (mayor) of the commote or the parish, who was a judge over his neighbours in matters of dispute, which frequently happened in that age. And it is all the more likely when we remember that a farm in almost every parish of Wales is called Maerdy, and notably so in agricultural parishes. Also in every incorporated city and town with their own charters, all over the country, the mayor has a house provided for him, and the mayor's court is used up to the present day for administering the law. The owner of this Maerdy once was Major Price, [6] the owner of the Baily-du Manor, and the holder was Mr William Price,[7] the owner of Tir Cwm Craf, a place

6 Major Price was Christopher Price who died in 1722.
He left three daughters and co-heirs, Rebecca, Wife of John Chambre ; Jane, wife of John Watkins, Ana unmarried ; Margaret, wife of William Bonner

7 Mr William Price was Great Grandfather of Mr Octavius Price, the owner of MS.

THE BLORENGE
Its tramroad and canal system
in the 19th century

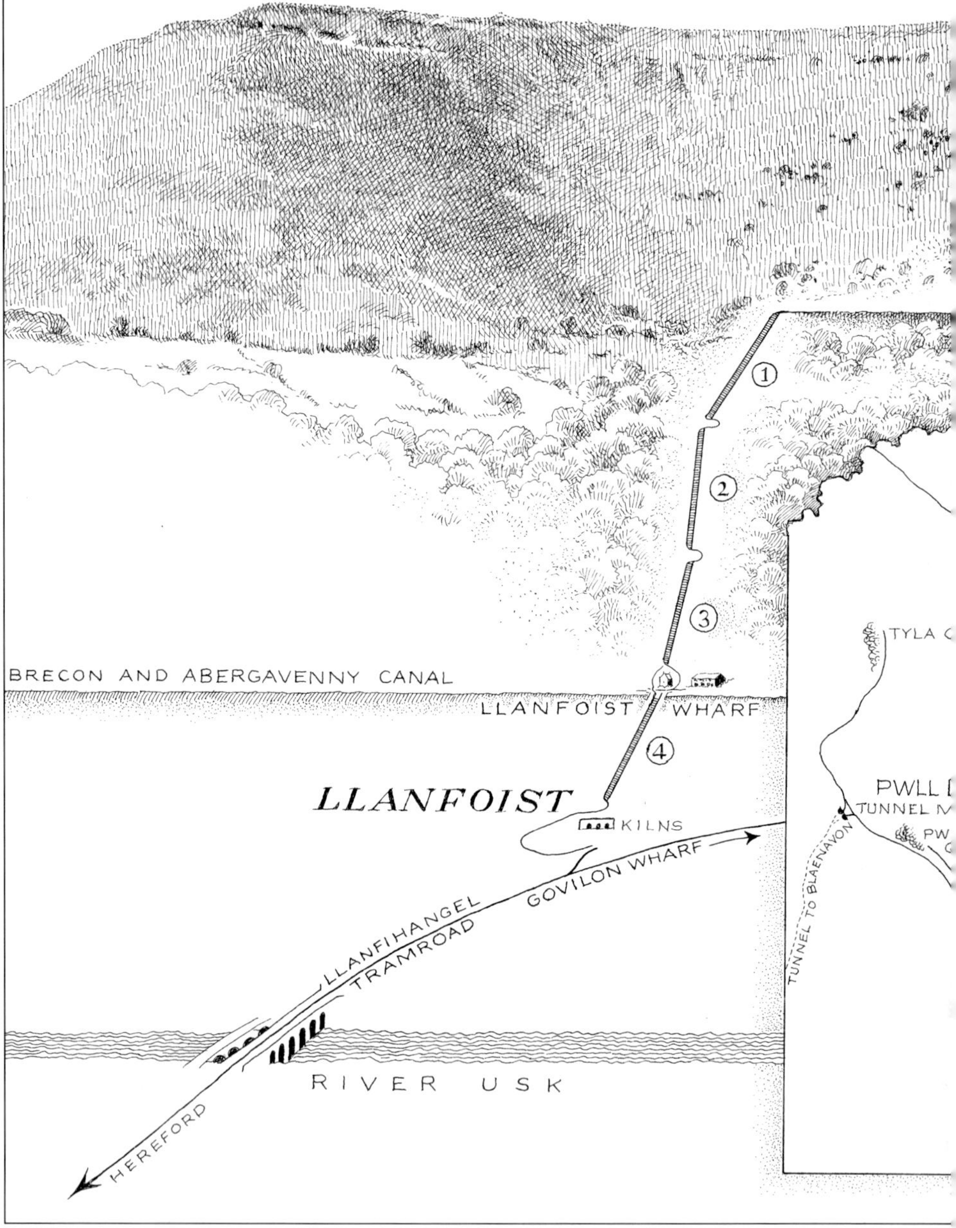

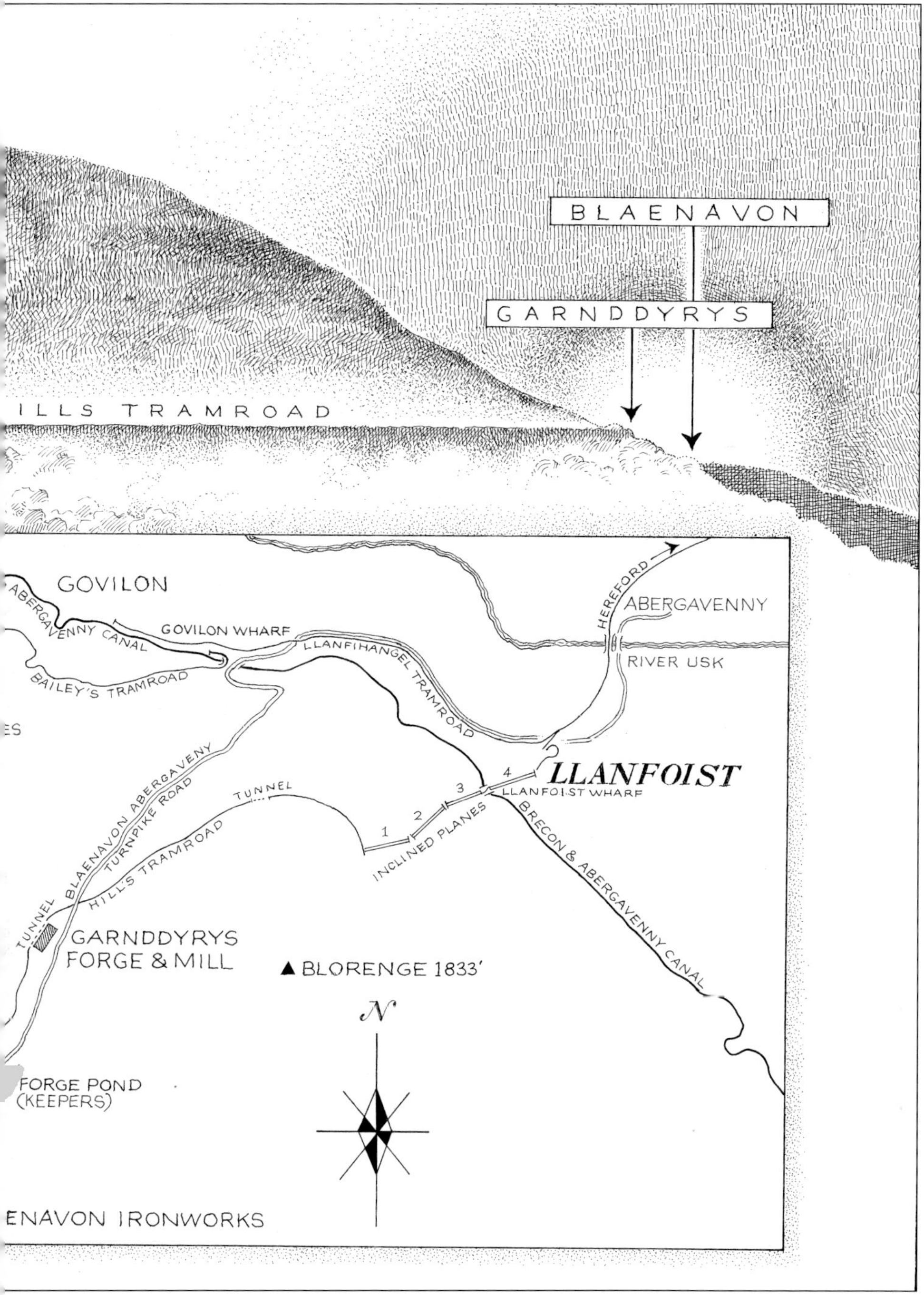
BLAENAVON
GARNDDYRYS
ILLS TRAMROAD
GOVILON
ABERGAVENNY CANAL
GOVILON WHARF
BAILEY'S TRAMROAD
LLANFIHANGEL TRAMROAD
HEREFORD
ABERGAVENNY
RIVER USK
ES
BLAENAVON ABERGAVENNY TURNPIKE ROAD
TUNNEL
HILL'S TRAMROAD
1
2
3
4
INCLINED PLANES
LLANFOIST
LLANFOIST WHARF
BRECON & ABERGAVENNY CANAL
TUNNEL
GARNDDYRYS FORGE & MILL
▲ BLORENGE 1833'
N
FORGE POND (KEEPERS)
ENAVON IRONWORKS

Looking down The 'Big Drop' - third section of the Llanfoist Incline.

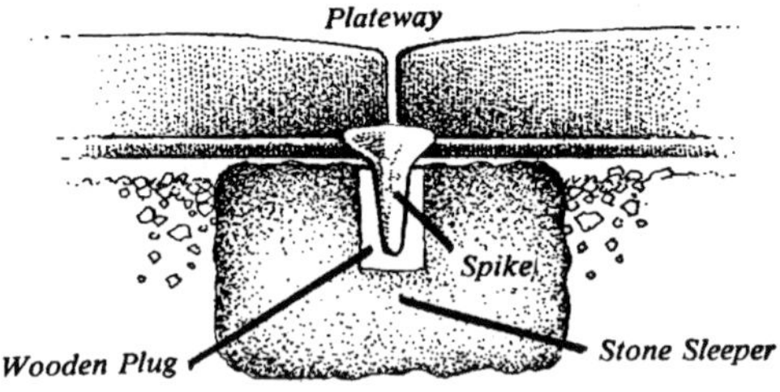

Detail of method of securing plateways.

we shall refer to again further on. Afterwards the Maerdy came into the possession of the eminent family of Coldbrook House, in the parish of Abergavenny, and after the death of the late J.H. Williams,[8] Esq., the Maerdy Farm was sold in parts at a public auction, and thus this fine old house and a small portion of the farm came into the possession of the late John Price [9] Esq., solicitor who converted the old house into a hostelry under the name of Waterloo, and built a part of the fine dwelling called Llanfoist Villa (where he afterwards lived and died) and also a number of comfortable houses on this land. His widow owns all this property, the daughter of the late Captain Chambre [10] of Upper Llanfoist (as his house was called), and the sister of the present Major Chambre,[11] the present owner of the place. On the Maerdy Farm near the old house, is the source of Nant Gryffydd (Griffiths Brook) which flows past the Parsonage to the river Usk under a small bridge called Pont Llan Gryffydd. On this farm were many large ponds , the work of the old monks who were keen on providing fish for their tables, and a man by the name of Morse caught lately the fish called tench in one of these lakes.

I shall now hasten on my tour, but before I proceed but very little on the parish road I find that the tram road here has its foundation on the parish road, with the old Maerdy Barn on the right hand and the field near to it sold to Mr. John Powell, who converted the barn into a dwelling house, and also sold several plots of the field to builders. As the tram road leaves the parish road it runs through a marshy glen and over a hillock, &c., on its sides many dwellings have been built by Messrs William Phillips, Daniel Davies, David Jones, James Cunoir, &c. The parish road winds on the left hand down to the side of the lake leaving it on the right hand, and on the left hand there are houses and a field and many luxuriant gardens, all on the Maerdy Farm, in the ownership of Mr John Lewis, ironmonger, Abergavenny. Having left the lake on the right hand, there is another part of the old Maerdy farm, the property of the late Mr James Cynfyn of Abergavenny, and having ascended from the road to the top of the hillock, there is on the left hand a piece of land, the property of Messrs, P.&B. Phillips of Llanwenarth, and another owned by Messrs, J.&C. Bailey

---

8. John Hanbury-Williams of Coldbrook died without issue. He was eldest son of George Hanbury-Williams by Margaret daughter of John Chambre by Rebecca, eldest daughter and co-heir of Christopher Price of Llanfoist. John Hanbury-Williams, dying without issue, was succeeded by his brother Ferdinand (born 1760, died 1810) from whom is descended the present family.

9. John Price of Abergavenny , solicitor married Jane Rebecca, daughter of Christopher Chambre of Llanfoist. He died in 1829, she died in 1844.

10. Christopher Chambre was Sheriff in 1784, died 1795.

11. Francis Chambre of Llanfoist, son of Christopher, liet-colonel R. Monmouth and Brecon Militia, died 1847.

The old Waterloo Inn, previously known as Maerdy Farm.

of Nantyglo. Passing on downwards, our feet are on the tram road, and we cross the road near the great bridge over the river Usk, and from which we get a clear view of the town of Abergavenny. There is another part of the farm again on the right hand called Cae'r Bedd (the field of the Grave) now owned by Mr John Rees, brewer, of Abergavenny. It is said that in this field were buried the bodies of those who died from the plague in Abergavenny. The oral tradition has been handed down to the present age, describing how they were conveyed in wagons and buried in their clothes, just as they appeared when death came on the scene, in large pits dug for the purpose, and about at the same time as that of the great plague in London. Another marvellous thing about this field is kept in remembrance viz.: when the reverend Mr Eustance, the clergyman of Abergavenny and Llanfoist, was one Sunday returning home on horseback, having officiated at this church, but living at that time in Abergavenny, a snake, huge in size, sprang from the field, over the hedge, the horse's back, the road, and the other hedge on the other side of the road, to the next field, which is enclosed with high walls by its owner Mr Bailey, where they burn lime, and sell it together with coal, to the farmers of Monmouth and Hereford. They convey their materials from their works in Nantyglo. And the limestones from Cwm-duar in Llanelly, over the tram road of their own construction to the Abergavenny and Brecon Canal in the parish of Llanwenarth, and from there over the tram road of Llanvihangel and Hereford to Tudor Bridge. We meet next on the right hand the Merthyr high road, and also a road to the Blaenavon Iron Works past a farm called Penybont, with several dwelling houses and gardens. It was the property of the late Mr Edward Edwards, but now owned by Mr Morgan Watkins. Between the afore-mentioned houses and the bridge opposite and the coal depot of Messers Bailey, is the place of the old great road of Govilon village leading to the bridge, but when the Llanvihangel and Hereford tram road was constructed this great road was closed, and there was a road made past the farm, the property of Lord Abergavenny, but in the hands of Thomas Hill, Esq. of Blaenavon, and a part of this road was closed, with nothing now but a footpath alone, and the ordinary road passing through Llanfoist village. There is an arch under the new bridge coming from the old road to Tudor Bridge, leading to, Abergavenny, on which I now stand. It was built by all account by one Jasper Tudor, Duke of Bedford, and Baron Abergavenny, in the reign of Henry VI. This is a strong bridge, but very narrow until recently when it was widened to the tramroad bridge. It has several arches over the river (see *Jones' Views in Wales),* and has been largely repaired and the road raised under the old dry bridge which was frequently covered by the flood, but now is almost always dry ground. The maintenance of this bridge rests with the authorities of the town of Abergavenny. When discussing this ancient bridge I may say that another has been usually mentioned between the two parishes (Abergavenny and Llanfoist), but lower down than this spot, near where the Cefnwy falls into the Usk. But there were some who doubted this until they found proof of it in a meadow near Abergavenny Castle. Since the year 1824 the river Usk inclines to the Castle Meadow, destroying and washing away a great deal of the land. And through this was revealed an old foundation wall of stone and mortar, pointing straight over the river, and this is the old road leading up to the castle and the town for the use of the people of Llanover, Llanelen, &c. It was also doubtless, the old path of Seisyllt ap Dyfnwallt from his palace in Llanover to Abergavenny.

From the Tudor Bridge there is a way under the Llanvihangel tramroad leading to the old Merthyr Tydfil road, opposite a portion of the Maerdy Farm in the possessions of Messrs. Bailey, [12] and further on there is on the right an old barn called by some Scubor Shoni Candy, but its old name is Ysgubor Yddallt. There are some who conjecture that the name is derived from Gwydd, small trees, and a cliff or precipice, meaning the Barn of the woody declivity, while others say it may be derived from Hydd and Gallt, that is, the Deer and Forest Barn, which is a more likely interpretation in view of the nature of the place.

We shall hasten on past some other portions of Maerdy Farm, owned by Major Chambre, and on the left there are other portions of the same farm, as mentioned already, held by Messrs. P&B Phillips. We shall reach, by walking only a few yards, the tops of these slopes, from which can be seen some fertile lands between the Great and Little Skyrrid, with the Sugar Loaf and Blorenge, and the river Usk meandering through the meadows with majestic grandeur. The Rectory road is on the left, leading to a farm of that name, which belongs to the living, and is owned by Lord Abergavenny, and now the residence of the Rev. W. Jones, who serves the parish, and not far from the church. Down the hollow from here runs Nant Gryffydd (*Griffiths Brook*), and on the right hand are two dwelling houses at one with the land of Pen-y-wrlod. Having crossed the bridge over the brook the fair and lovely farm of Pen-y-wrlod spreads its gorgeous view before us, and the house stands on a lofty upland, well in sight of Abergavenny. It is owned by Major Chambre, and is the residence of his sister, Mrs Price, already mentioned. Not far away we meet again with the Merthyr mail road, and the old parish road, on the left hand from Abergavenny and Llanfoist, crossed by the Llanvihangel tramroad. The broad acres of Cadvor Farm (or perhaps Cadivor) are on the right hand, the property of F.S.L.W. Secretan [13] Esq. Of Llandeilo Portholeu, and the division of Llanfoist parish is on this farm, running down to the river Usk. When we ascend the Glydfas

12. Joseph (afterwards Sir Joseph, bart) and Crawshay Bailey of Nantyglo.

13.This gentleman's full name at this period was Frederick Samuel Secretan-James-Woodhouse. He was originally Frederick Samuel Secretan, and built the house which he called Arcadia, now known as Triley Court. He assumed the additional surnames of James-Woodhouse in 1817.

(*cosy field*) we come within sight of Dolfawr, Upper Llanfoist, and there is a fine mansion built on the part below the Canal. When passing over the road towards the church, leaving Pen-y-wrlod on the left hand, we are opposite the palace where Robert Wheeley, [14] Esq. lives, part proprietor of the Blaenavon Iron Works. This place [15] was once in the ownership of Dr Christopher Price, a renowned physician about the year 1653 to 1687, when he died and was buried in the chancel, in front of the communion table, at St. Mary's Church Abergavenny. He was also a gifted minister of genius with the Baptists at Abergavenny, and a great assistance to them in many ways, presenting them with a quadrangular piece of land near the village of Govilon in the parish of Llanwenarth, to build a place of worship on it. The number of children he left I do not know, but I am aware of one daughter, who married Colonel Chambre,[16] who built the palace which now stands, and they had four, if not more, children. One son of theirs died in his youth. The youngest daughter married George Hanbury, Esq., and the present family of Coldbrook is descended from their lineage (*Coxe*, 244). The other son was the late Captain Chambre, who had two sons and a daughter, and the elder son is the present Major Chambre. It is of this palace that Cox said in his historical tour through Monmouthshire in 1800 (P.172) :- "On leaving the town through Tudor Gate, holding the glass in my hand, how great is the glory which spreads before me, such as the Usk flowing gently along under the arches of the bridge, through the rich meadow land, and Upper Llanfoist House as if embosomed in a rich grove of oak trees, &c. with Blorenge robed in its majestic garb, towering in the immensity's above. A more glorious combination of picturesque scenes were never grouped together for the eyes of men to behold. And together they produce such an effect on the feelings that neither pen nor pencil can adequately describe."

The height of the Blorenge was determined by General Roy to be 1720 feet higher than the river Cenfi where it flows to the Usk, opposite the meadows of the farm land in this parish (*Cox* 266). The tramroad of Llanvihangel is on the left, opposite the palace of Major Chambre, and on the edge of the parish road. We can see the church here, and a road on the left leading to the parsonage and towards Abergavenny, &c., also a hostelry built on the ruins of what was once considered an old monastery, and the place, with the adjoining land, was called Tir Syr Siarls (*Sir Charles Land*), and was subsequently a part of the Maerdy Farm, but was sold in portions at the same time as Maerdy, and the foundations of the old house and a

---

14. Robert Wheeley married daughter of Rev. James Jenkins, mentioned before.
15. This house is that known as Llanfoist-house or Ty-mawr.
16. This is not correct. Dr. Christopher Price had a son Christopher, father of Rebecca, wife of John Chambre.

field belonging to it, came to the possession of Mr James Jones, who built an inn and a beer brewery here. If the old building had ever been a monastery, it supports the theory that the lakes already mentioned on the Maerdy Farm existed at the same time. What makes me think that the old house was connected with the church is the name Sir Charles, for frequently in the olden times the parochial clergy were called Sir A. or Sir B.

There is a road on the right hand, and also the brook of Cwm Craf which dries up instantly after crossing these roads, between the inn and the churchyard, at the lower gate of the entrance to the church, &c. From the church there is a road which leads to the place where the old parish mill stood, and after starting there from the churchyard we leave the Maerdy road on the left, and having crossed the tramroad of T. Hill & Co., we find on the right hand dwelling houses and land owned by Thomas Harris. On our way forward on the left hand there is a road from Tudor Bridge and then land called The Farm. We proceed just a little onward and find the gate of Middle Llanfoist Farm, [17] which used to be the property of Mr Proger of Wernddu, in the parish of Llandeilo Petholeu, afterwards owned by the late Richard Lee Esq., and now by his daughters, one of which is the widow of the late John Jones, Esq. Of Llanarth Court, and the other I not know where she is. They are the present owners, and their tenant is Mr William Watkins. There is a road which leads from the house of Penref Bach, a farm owned by F.H. Williams, [18] Esq. Of Coldbrook, and a road further on, and on the right hand a branch leading to the mounting land of the parish, and to Blaenavon, by Castell Prydydd. A little further on we find on the left hand a gate opening to the old palace and farm of Baily Du. [19] Baily and Bailiau were commonly used in the North and South to describe places in olden times meaning a court or enclosure.

---

17. Middle Llanfoist (Llanffwyst Ganol') was the seat of a family named Williams, descended from Howel y Coed, brother of Sir David Gam. The last of this family was Walter Williams, who left a daughter and heir, Elizabeth, wife of Edward Proger of Wernddu. Their son William Proger sold the estate to Richard Lee. Richard Lee of Great Delce, Kent and of Clytha and Middle Llanfoist (Llanffwyst Ganol) came into this county through his marriage, in 1767, with Mary, daughter of John Jones of Llanarth. He had three daughters and co-heirs. Mary married her cousin, John Jones of Llanarth, Elizabeth was unmarried, Apollonia married Robert Berkeley of Spetchley, co. Worcester.

18. Ferdinand Hanbury-Williams.

19. Beili-du is the house called Lower Llanfoist, now used as the premises of a golf club. Around it are remains of extensive gardens, fish ponds, etc., with a park wall along the road leading from Llanfoist to Llanelen.

There was a manor and a large, fine estate attached to Baily Du in the days of old, owned by Major Prys and his daughter Anne who married John Hanbury [20] (See *Cox*, 244). And in that way it is supposed it became the property of the ancestors of F.H. Williams Esq. of Coldbrook House. Baily Du was an extremely fine old building, with a large fishpond before it. And in close proximity there is a white thorn, very much noted, which blossoms every night before the old Christmas Day, and only then according to some, while others say it blossoms every night during the Christmas Holidays. There are many strange things imagined about this thorn : for instance, when Joseph of Arimathea came to preach the gospel in Britain, that once upon a time he struck his staff into the earth in the Isle of Affallon in Somersetshire, and that it at once took root, grew and blossomed a great forest tree, and that this famous white thorn is a part of it. Whatever may be the truth there is much resorting to it at those special times already mentioned. Another remarkable thing mentioned in connection with this farm, and still remembered is the following:

About 1780, a gentleman lived here who had a daughter who favoured a married man at Abergavenny with her friendship, in spite of her father, and it was carried on clandestinely. But one dark night the woman was found missing, and after the lapse of several days found drowned, with her body in the lake, under circumstances suspicious that she was possibly wilfully drowned by the wretch, because there was the impression of a man's foot on the edge of the lake. But there were others who said she must have fallen into the lake, her foot slipping when crossing from the field near the garden on leaving her lover.

We pass the gate on the road on to the end of the parish, and a small brook divides the parish of Llanelen from Llanfoist. It was here that the old Manor Mill stood, but is not here now, nor any dwelling either. From here the road goes to Llanelen village, the towns of Usk, Pontypool, &c. We now leave the plain and go further up, to behold a view of the whole valley already mentioned, with beautiful meadows fair to look upon, fertile fields, blooming orchards. Pine trees of stately growth, with animals and cattle to bless the country side abundantly. We also see the roads and tramroads, bridges. &c. Returning to the Blaenavon road and following it we come to the canal of Brecon, Abergavenny and Newport-on-Usk, and two dwellings, and on the left is the farm of Castell Prydydd, another portion of the inheritance of F.H. Williams, Esq. This farm is made up of a large and considerable

---

20. John Hanbury, eldest son of John Hanbury of Pontypool, M.P. (and brother of George Hanbury-Williams, who married Miss Chambre) married Anne, daughter of Thomas Price of Llanfoist, and had an only child Anne, died in infancy. She married secondly Herbert Tryst, and died in 1784, aged 71. She seems to have been the last of the family to reside at Beili-du or Lower Llanfoist.

number of small holdings, whose names have now been lost. The castle was built by one of the owners (at least renovated) of Coldbrook, viz.: Sir Charles Hanbury Williams, [21] an eminent English poet in his day, in the 17th century, who once greatly roused the anger of the Irish by satirising them in his poetry.

A little further on the right we find the road of Tylau Crwn (Round Slopes) leading to the farm of Tylau Crwn, Neuadd Penygraig, Cwm Craf, Cwnhingen Gaer, and a road on the right leading from the church through the parson's wood and on to the summit of the Blorenge. Having left the open of Tylau Crwn road, and on the old Blaenavon road, crossing a small brook which flows from the bottom of Cwm y Disan, called by the English Punchbowl, we proceed to the farm of Nindda Isaf, that once belonged to a family of Joneses, afterwards to B. Jacob and Samuel Hopkins, Esq., one of the founders of the Blaenavon Iron Works and afterwards his sister, Miss Sarah Hopkins,[22] but now to Mr Abraham Rosser. A few years ago there was a smelting iron furnace here owned by one Hawkins, but it is not here now. There is another farm near, the property of Walter Wilkins Esq., Maesllwch, in Radnorshire, and on again in the same direction, and on the same hand, there is the farm of Upper Nindda, owned by Mr John Jenkins, and a cross road before it called the road of Fuddau, dividing the parishes of Llanfoist and Llanelen, and it runs down to the brook which flows by the old Mill. Immediately on a few paces the Blaenavon road winds to the mountain : and on the right hand a cross road winds around the farm of Upper Nindda, leaving the parish of Llanelen on the left, and travelling on this road to the top of the hillocks, we see the exquisite beauty of the clovery valley beneath. Shortly the Blaenavon road comes near on the left and runs jointly to Coed-cae'r-gorfydd on the right, in the parish of Llanfoist, leaving Cefn Goleu and Cefn y Gylchen, Pwll Mawddwy and Pe-y-ffordd-goch, until it comes to the upper part of the parish.

The road of Cwmcraf leads up from the church (by an old building, now dwelling houses, the property of Mr Walter Edwards of Llandeilo Porteleu), under the arch of the canal, rising to the tramroad aforementioned and the upper edge of the canal and the rectory wood. Here the road divides into two, the left hand leading to the Graig Fawr (Great Rock) and Graig Dew (Thick Rock), owned by Lord Abergavenny, and then, turning to the right, we pass up through the parson's wood to the farms of Tir Cwm Craf, the property of the late Mr William Price of Maerdy, but now of his son Mr B Price of Abergavenny. There are other farms called Penygraig, Neuadd, &c., owned by the late John Hanbury Williams, Esq., of Coldbrook, but now by his nephew, Ferdinand H. Williams, Esq. Of the same place.

---

21. Sir Charles Hanbury-Williams, K.B., son of John Hanbury of Pontypool, M.P.
22. Miss Sarah Hopkins founded the school at Blaenavon, for the endowment of which she settled the sum of £3,000.

The other part of the road is on the right hand side, leading through a part of the parson's wood to the Great Forest of Captain Chambre, and again the parson's wood, ascending to the farm of Gwning-gaer aforementioned, and on to Pen-y-graig farm, owned by F.S.S. Woodhouse, Esq. of Arcadia [23] in Llandeilo Pertholeu, and from there climbing through the steepy woodlands to the top of Cwm Craf. Having reached the stile, and climbed to the side of the Blorenge, we wind our way, or rather creep with much difficulty on the sides of this dingle, the height of which was taken by an air-weighing machine in the year 1787, and proved to be 1607 feet 5 inches (*Williams History*) from a field on the bank of the Usk at Abergavenny. (*Wilson*).

Tunnel beneath the canal at Llanfoist

23. Now called Triley Court.

In times of persecution it is said that people were placed on top of this valley in a kind of wooden barrel, tied and closed up, the barrel penetrated with nails, then rolled topsy turvy, headlong down to the bottom. Large beds of limestone come to the surface here, and there are scores of round pits deep and waterless on the side of the Blorenge, and some say it is impossible to find out their original purpose, unless they were made to provide safe hiding places for the old Silurians when driven by the Romans, the Anglo-Saxons and the Normans (*History of Monmouthshire*). There are similar pits in adjoining parishes, viz.: Llanwenarth, Llanelen, Llanover, Trevethin, &c., and some of them are called by the name of "Disgwylfa," observatory or watchtower. But I must state my own opinion of the pits, although I doubt not that they were useful to the ancient Welsh in their wars with the aliens which persecuted them. We know this from their present names, possibly preserved from those olden times. Most people know of the large caves that abound everywhere in limestone beds, and that scarcely any of those hollows are found except where the limestones come to the surface. Doubtless many of them sunk in the time of the deluge to the position in which they are now seen. The same thing takes place today when heavy rains come pouring down incessantly, the earth falls in and huge vacant spaces appear, and in time one would think they were constructed by men, but they are not in my judgement.

I shall now proceed to the highest peak of Corlan Gwilym Meredith, the height of which has been found (through an air Weigher in 1787) to be 1720 feet and 4 inches above the river Usk ; and from the summit of this high mountain are seen with the naked eye, all Monmouthshire, Hereford, Gloucester and Brecknock, a part of Glamorgan and Worcester, the Severn and its ships, Somerset, &c. Many of the old Silurians fled to these mountains when driven from their country by the Romans and Saxons, &c. (History of Abergavenny). And here afterwards lived without ever being conquered. These brave tribes of mountaineers from the Usk to the Rhymney, which is the old province or kingdom of "Glwysig," or "Glewysig" (*Williams' History*) were never at any time subdued by, or brought in any way under the yoke of, the foreign invaders.

There is a plentiful supply on these mountains of wimberries and meadow cherries. I must now bid adieu to the fair domains of meadow land and valley in this parish, to make a brief enquiry to the old notabilities (at least the descendants of those who were great in their day), besides those I have already mentioned since I began this project, such as the old family of Williams, Llanfoist, which I mentioned at the outset. I received my information about the lineage from a learned friend at Abergavenny W. Price Esq., Solicitor, who writes as follows .... (several lines have been omitted here which are merely quotations from Williams' History of Monmouthshire).

I must now leave the banks of the Usk and bid them farewell for a short time. I leave the fertile fields so full of clover, the flowery meadows and all the tuneful tribe who warble so melodiously in the gorgeous groves, to climb to the mountain top above the little cot of my father and mother, where I was born and reared by my parents. I now come to where I left, viz.: by Coed Cae'r Gorfydd and to Cefn y Gylchen, and through the end of Rhas Fach to Pwll Mawddwy and Pen y Ffordd Goch. There is no richer land in the whole of the principality than the end of the valley of Avon Lwyd (Torfaen), that is to say, the upper part of the parish of Llanfoist. When on Pen y Ffordd Goch there is a road leading down to the Blaenavon Works and to Pontypool. On the right hand are the roads of Garnddryrys, y Pwlldu and Llanelly, and the ordinary parish road leading from the Llanelen way to the end of the river Torfaen (Blaen yr afon Torfaen) and over to Blaenau Gwent. There are hundreds of grouse around these mountains, and hundreds of gentry who come annually from all parts of the kingdom to enjoy great happiness in shooting them.

I pass onto a place called Croes Ifor, where we find the top of the road to Llanwenarth valley joining the old road to Llanfoist, and not far from the remains of an old Castle called Ifor's Castle, in the parish of Llanwenarth, and from here near the summit of Twyn Du by Carreg Maen Taraw to the junction of Monmouthshire and Breconshire, and over the hill on Carn yr Erw (perhaps in olden times Carn Arw) to the road of Coety Mawr, and the top of Coety, where the parishes of Blaenau and Llanfoist join. We move on from here above the house of Mr David Davies, to the side of the stone fence and down to the upper end of Nant Oerna which divides Trevethin and Llanfoist, by the house of Lewis Roberts, esq. formerly, now owned by the Blaenavon Iron Co., and across by the house of Mr Thomas Deakin on the other side of the mountain, and up through a place called Rhas y Cadben to the old parish road, and back to Coed Ifor. Our nearest house now on the middle of the high mountain is the old residence of one Abram Harry, who cut the coal to fill hundreds of sacks to supply the country long before the time of tramroads and canals. The farmers in the counties of Monmouth and Hereford brought their wagons to Pwlldu, y Rhas Newydd and Cwm Llammarch in Breconshire to bring the coal back to their homes. Their roads passed through a place called Gilwern in the parish of Llanwenarth, and down over the steep declivity to the village of Govilon. It was not usual in those days to see scores and hundreds of mules loaded with sacks of coal and lime to supply the needs of the residents of Abergavenny and the country around.

I shall now move on through the peaty marshes and over the ore works of Pinau Duon to the old house of Carn yr Erw, to which a recent addition has been made, and a row of new houses has been built lately by the Blaenavon Iron Co., but now in a dilapidated condition. The coal industry was once very flourishing here and a tramroad was made to the smelting furnaces of Blaenavon, passing by the row of workmen's houses. I shall return by the coal pits, which have now been worked for a few years with an output of scores of tons daily, and the machinery worked by hydraulic power. I reach the house of Miss Mary Lewis [24] who owned much land, now the property of Blaenavon Iron Co. This lady was a sister of the late L. Roberts, Esq., and one of the most virtuous and benevolent in her day to the poor and destitute and to religious causes of all persuasions. Although her body is mouldering in the dust her name is still remembered with the greatest of respect and affection by all her acquaintances. She was the aunt of the present Walter Lewis. [25] Esq., of Bryn y cwm, in the parish of Llanwenarth.

There are pits to raise ore on the banks of the Torfaen which are in full work and moved by hydraulic power from the river Torfaen which runs through a trench constructed for this purpose on the lower side of Mr James Brown's house (formerly Miss M. Lewis's.) There are also, a little higher up on the same land, pits to raise ore and coal.

There are several old houses between here and Blaen y cwm, used by the inhabitants of this district before the works were started here. They are now crumbling away because of the elements beating upon them through the ceaseless rush of the years, and the old inhabitants have been long removed to the land of silence and forgetfulness, while others are populating the district and entering into its inheritance.

Quite near is the dwelling of the late renowned old Welshman in his day, Mr Daniel David Morgan, who passed away full of years, over 80, and was buried at Llanwenarth. On the other side of the river is Rectory Farm, but is commonly known by the name of Tir Rhisiart Shon. This place was bought by Samuel Hopkins, Esq., who presented it for the use of Blaenavon Church, now held by the Reverend Jas. Jenkins, the minister of the place. There is an old building not far from here, the house of the late Gwilym Rasur Edmund, whose widow lives here now. Very much land is owned by that family and divided by the sons and daughters. A portion of it is held by one Mr Richard Roberts, reaching to the mountain on each side of the river Torfaen, full of ore and coal, with liberty over a great deal of the mountain for cattle, sheep, &c. upon which the whole of the farmers of these mountainous regions depend for their sustenance.

---

24. Miss Mary Lewis was a daughter of William Lewis of Trevethin, son of Francis of Llanover, son of Richard Lewis of Danyparc, co. Brecon, Esq. Her brother, William Lewis, was father of Edward Lewis of Blaenavon, father of the late Mr. Ebenezer Lewis of Maindy, Newport, and of Mr. Benjamin Lewis of Glanbaiden.
25. Walter Lewis was son of Walter (brother of Miss Mary Lewis) and brother of William Lewis of Ty-hir in Llantilio Pertholey.

Carreg Maen Taro, above Pwll-du

Leaving this place we shall pass on to various houses old and new until we come to Rhiw y Coety Mawr, which divides the parish of Llanfoist from the parish of Blaenau Gwent on the summit of Coety mountain. We now come to the Coety Farm which is held by copyhold by Mr Harry Jenkins, and we pass on through the meadows and Coedcae y Vedw (*Beechwood)* to the Coety Mawr held by Mr Dd. Davies and owned by the Blaenavon Co. Striding back through the heather mounds and wilderness and over the uplands, we come to Ffawydden Farm, owned by the Blaenavon Co. and held by Mr Misael Morgan, and then to the house of Mr William Whitney, and others of less note.

All the lands in this part of the parish of Llanfoist are of no value for producing corn because of their high altitude ; they only rear sheep, young cattle, and milching cows, out of which the inhabitants make an ample living. The surface of the soil is usually peat and sticky clay, not congenial for growing any valuable crops, but good for making bricks and coarse earthenware vessels. But this is only a trifle when contrasted with the enormous wealth of iron ore and coal, limestone, &c. deposited in the depths of this most precious part of Gwent uwch Coed. The old Welshmen of Blaen Torfaen once owned the whole of this commote and its contents, but because of their benighted ignorance, and on account of the aforesight and enterprise of the Englishmen, all these precious minerals were cunningly taken away from the old natives racy of the soil, for a million times less than their true value. And the descendants of those hardy old true mountaineers, whose renown has passed away, are now of no more account than others.

The old Welshmen who inhabited the parish used to compare the parish of Llanfoist to an hour glass, very wide at both extremities but narrow in the middle. And a better description could never be given by any surveyor or artistic designer in the world, for, as we previously observed, its lower part extends from the parish of Llanelen to the parish of Llanwenarth, for nearly two miles on the banks of the river Usk, and narrows until it is not much wider than a footpath at Coedcae Carn y Gorfydd and over Cefn y Gylchen, Pwll Mawddwy, Peny y Ffordd Goch, &c. On to Croes Ifor. Here it begins to widen over the Twyn Du to Carreg Maen Taraw to where it joins Breconshire ; and it extends from the parish of Llanelly in Breconshire to the parish of Trevethin in Monmouthshire, that is to say, for nearly two miles. Concerning the place called Carn yr Erw, the reader will probably desire more knowledge because of the name. There are some who believe that there was a Druidical heap of stones here in the far-off days of the ancient Druids. Others think that that Carn arw (*Rugged Mound*) is the correct name, and the most appropriate because the place is full of rough stones, and a wilderness to cover the whole ground, so that Carn arw certainly would be no misnomer. To my Knowledge there are many places called Carn in the neighbouring districts, such as Carn y cadnaw (*The Fox's mound*) in the parish of Blaneau, Carnddyrys (*Entangled mound* Carn y

Blawreang (*The Blorenge mound*) in the parish of Llanwenarth, Carn y clochdy (*The Steeple mound*), and Carn ddiffaeth (*The Desert mound*) in the parish of Trevethin, and many more I could mention. I know from personal observation that all such places are full of rough stones in huge piles but full of disorder and confusion, so that it appears to me not to be improbable that Carn arw was its primitive name, like other mounds in the neighbourhood.

This parish contains an abundance of almost all things for the necessities of man and beast, such as the richest and finest fields for crops and produce in the whole of Gwent. There are corn, barley, oats, rye, peas, potatoes, turnips, and all kinds of garden produce, and a variety of fruits, which are sent to supply the needs of the inhabitants of Nantyglo, Beaufort, and the works of Great Ebbwy, Tredegar, &c. The white clover and the primroses grow in the fields of this parish and on the ridge of the mountains. Thousands of exquisite flowers beautify its meadows and decorate its dales in rich exuberance. And all this is not only ornamental but also useful, for its affords pasture for the mountain sheep and the lambs which gambol around with delightful innocency. Here also the grouse and the larks fly and sing at early dawn on the slopes of the Blorenge, all of which I see and hear as I stand on the top of Corlan (*sheepfold*) Gwilym Meredith. And the dawn in spring and summer spreads its light a long time before the inhabitants of these commotes perceive its broad wings of golden tint appearing.

The richest mines owned by the Blaenavon Iron Co. are in this parish, for all the veins of the ore and coal run under the upper part of it, from what is described as Pin gwaelod to Gloyn briglwyd, or the highest in the earth, and next to Maen Fo. Who can conceive the vast treasures that are concealed in this parish? It is a much greater achievement than I can adequately accomplish. I will say this in conclusion, that this parish is one of the finest and most curious of all regions within the range of my knowledge. And the unrivalled scenery observed from the summits of its lofty heights is always first and foremost in attracting the attention of the stranger when coming to Abergavenny and the neighbourhood around. O precious field!, your minerals underneath have enriched hundreds of men renowned for their wealth. I must now conclude, craving your forgiveness for the length of my tract and the researches of my travels, which I collected through much trouble and disadvantage, assuring you of my joy if you think they merit your least attention, and are of the smallest benefit to your honourable Society ; also praying for a long life to the President, our Patron, and all concerned, in the bonds of love, unity, truth and brotherhood. I remain, with all good wishes, your sincere friend until death.

Gwgan ap Bleddyn
September 27th 1834.

OTHER TITLES PUBLISHED BY BLORENGE BOOKS

Blorenge Books publish books about Wales and in particular the area covered by the ancient kingdom of Gwent. Copies of the following titles may be obtained by writing to Blorenge Books and enclosing cheques (made out to Blorenge Books) for the stated amounts. Please add £1 per book for postage.

Walks in Cordell Country
by Chris Barber (ISBN 1 872730 116 - £6)

Classic Walks in the Brecon Beacons National Park
by Chris Barber (ISBN 87230 08 6 - £8.95

Arthurian Caerleon
by Chris Barber (ISBN 1 87 2730 10 8 - £3.99)

The Ancient Stones of Wales
by Chris Barber and John Williams
(ISBN 0 9510444 7 8 - £7.95)

In Search of Owain Glyndwr
by Chris Barber (ISBN 1 872730 07 8 - £11.95)

Stone and Steam in the Black Mountains
by David Tipper (ISBN 0 9510444 1 9 - £5.75)

We Shall Sing Again
by Marguerite Shaw (ISBN 1 872730 00 0 - £6)

Shall We Meet Again?
by Marguerite Shaw (ISBN 1 872730 0 9 - £4.75)

Valley of Shadows
by Charles Hawkins (ISBN 1 872730 14 0 - £4.95)

Rape of the Fair Country
by Alexander Cordell (ISBN 1 872730 15 9 - £5.99)

Hosts of Rebecca
by Alexander Cordell (ISBN 1872730 19 1 - £5.99)

Blorenge Books, Blorenge Cottage, Church Lane, Llanfoist, Abergavenny NP7 9NG (Tel: 01873 856114)